THE WEAPONS ENCYCLOPÆDIA

TANK AIRCRAFT AFV SHIP ARTILLERY VEHICLES SECRET WEAPON

ITALIAN LIGHT TANKS L3/33-35-38

THE WEAPONS ENCYCLOPÆDIA

PUBLISHED BY

Luca Cristini Editore (Soldiershop), via Orio, 35/4 - 24050 Zanica (BG) ITALY.

DISTRIBUTION BY

Soldiershop - www.soldiershop.com, Amazon, Ingram Spark, Berliner Zinnfigurem (D), LaFeltrinelli, Mondadori, Libera Editorial (Spain), Google book (eBook), Kobo, (eBoook), Apple Book (eBook).

CONTRIBUTORS IN THIS ISSUE & ACKNOWLEDGEMENTS

First contributors to this book: Ruggero Calò author of the profiles he signed (the others are all by author Luca Cristini), Aymeric Lopez, Paolo Crippa and Luca Cristini. Special thanks to institutions such as: Stato Maggiore dell'esercito, Archivio di Stato, Bundesarchiv, Nara, Library of Congress, Wikipedia, USAF, Signal magazine, Cronache di guerra, Fronte di guerra, IWM, Australian War Museum, ecc. A P.Crippa, A.Lopez, L.Manes, C.Cucut, archivi Tallillo. Model Victoria (www.modelvictoria.it) ecc.

For a complete list of Soldiershop titles, or for every information please contact us on our website: www.soldiershop.com or www. cristinieditore.com. E-mail: info@soldiershop.com. Keep up to date on Facebook & Twitter: https://www.facebook.com/soldiershop. publishing

Title: **ITALIAN LIGHT TANKS CV L3/33-35-38** Code.: **TWE-001 EN** Series edited by L. S. Cristini
ISBN code: 978-88-9328669. First edition September 2022

THE WEAPONS ENCYCLOPAEDIA (SOLDIERSHOP) is a trademark of Luca Cristini Editore

ITALIAN LIGHT TANKS CV L3/33-35-38

SERIES EDITED BY LUCA STEFANO CRISTINI

BOOK SERIES FOR MODELERS & COLLECTORS

CONTENTS

▼ Front and back view of a light tank recently exhibited at Novegro (MI)-Militalia.

INTRODUCTION

Created in the early 1930s to supply the Italian army with a large-scale light tank, the L3 remained at the forefront of armoured units until 1941. Although it only played an important role in the fighting of the Ethiopian campaign and the Spanish Civil War, the *'sardine box'* was later limited to anti-partisan combat and support of occupation troops after the difficult start of the Second World War.

Due to its characteristics, the **L33** or **CV33** light tank was better known to Italian soldiers as the *'sardine box'*, *'steel coffin'* or *'death box'*; not very reassuring names given by Italian tank drivers to what was intended, in the intentions of the Italian high command at the start of the Second World War, to be an assault tank.

Even the term 'light tank' today appears to be an understatement (even the Sherman was considered a light tank, and weighed a good 30 tonnes compared to just over 3 of the early L3s).

The fast tank was certainly the most famous and well-known among Italian tanks of all time. In spite of its meagre war capabilities, it was widely used on all war fronts where the Royal Italian Army was engaged. Produced in large numbers considering the country's industrial capacity in the 1930s, around 2,000 examples were built from 1933 until 1938, when production ceased.

▼ This photo of an L 3/35 from the 32nd Rgt. of the Ariete Division in North Africa gives a good idea of the size of the Italian light tank.

▲ Wooden model presented by Ansaldo in 1929. It is very far from the prototype's forms.

THE DEVELOPMENT

In 1928, General Cavallero, then Undersecretary of War, decided to equip the Regio Esercito with a light reconnaissance tank to accompany the infantry. The British *Carden-Loyd Mk. VI* tankette caught the attention of the Technical Automotive Inspectorate, which decided to test it in Italy. As the results were not entirely satisfactory, the Ansaldo company was commissioned to develop a more suitable variant in line with the Italian army's expectations.

Ansaldo began by building a wooden model that was presented in 1929. The prototype light tank, very different from the model, was built in 1930 by engineer Rosini.

Its rolling train was inspired by the *Carden-Loyd*, but it had three pairs of wheels on each side instead of two. However, the body and superstructure were enlarged to accommodate a more powerful engine and to improve habitability. The vehicle was intended to tow a two-axle tracked trailer.

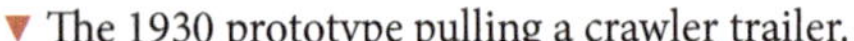

▼ The 1930 prototype pulling a crawler trailer.

ITALIAN LIGHT TANKS L3/33-35-38

▲ The prototype of the armored transport on the left, and that of the light tank on the right.

As the chassis suspension was unsatisfactory, Ansaldo modified the undercarriage of the prototype in 1931; a guide roller was added in front of the tensioning wheel.

A second prototype was also built for battlefield supply, without a roof and with a redesigned cogwheel. This armoured transport prototype was tested at the same time as the standard tank and served as the basis for further developments.

After testing near Genoa, a pre-series of four was ordered in 1932. On these vehicles, the original water-cooled Fiat mod.14 6.5 mm machine gun was replaced by an air-cooled Fiat mod.14 aviation gun. Front mudguards were also added, two headlights and the side grilles were moved to the sides of the cockpit.

TECHNICAL CHARACTERISTICS

The tank consisted of the chassis (or hull), the armament, the engine and its transmission, locomotion and control components. The vehicle had a mass of 3.2 tonnes. It was 3.17 metres long, 1.4 metres wide and 1.3 metres high.

The hull: it consisted of steel plates rigidly connected so as to form a non-deformable complex. The armour plating ranged from a minimum of 6 to 14 mm and provided sufficient protection from bullets fired from rifles and machine guns, shrapnel or minor artillery hits. It consisted of two side walls, a front, a rear and an upper wall, a bottom and a turret.

Two bulkheads divided the inside of the hull into three chambers. Starting from the first at the front of the craft, we have: the combat chamber, the engine chamber, and finally, at the rear, the one for the cooling organs. In the first one we find: the crew, composed of two people (tank leader on the left and pilot on the right), the armament, the transmission and control organs and the fuel tank, in the second, the engine and, in the third, the radiator. The turret includes several plates: in one of the front plates there is a casemate housing for the weapons and in another there is an opening, closed by a flap, for the pilot's forward view; the upper one has two openings - for the entry and exit of the two crew members - that can be closed with flaps; in the

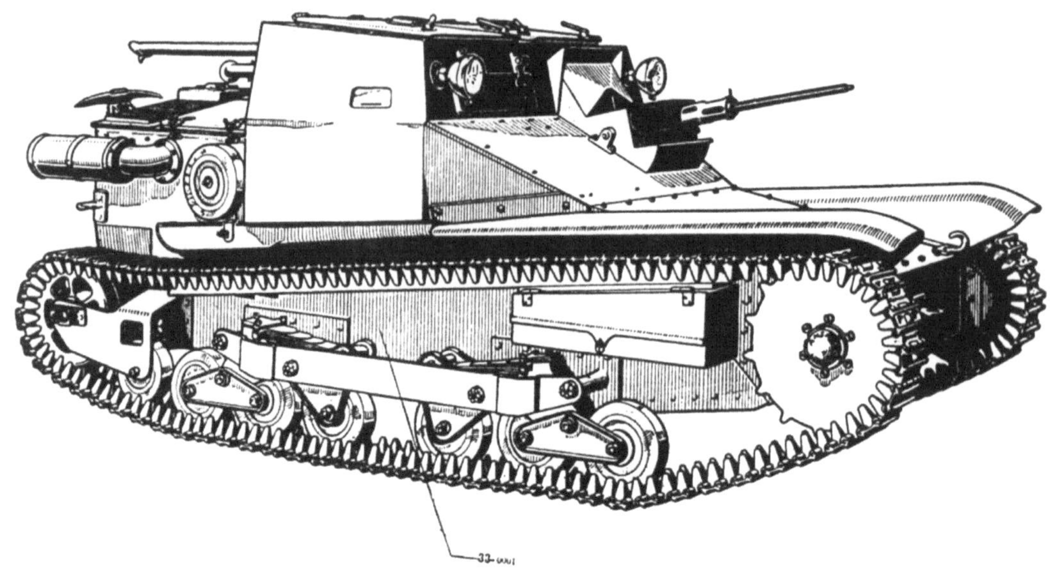

▲ Drawing of the CV 33 series 1. Note the toolbox latch, the shuttle on the side of the cab, and the common support for the guide roller and tension wheel.

rear one there are also two openings, with flaps, for the rear view. Slits for the side view were also added on the later versions.

Armament: the most common weaponry consisted of two paired Fiat cal. 8 machine guns, or a Fiat cal. 8 machine gun, or a flamethrower: all were housed in a mobile casemate, by means of a cradle and retaining pin. They were loaded and manoeuvred from inside the cockpit by the tank master.

The installation provided the weapons with a horizontal firing sector of 40° (20° to the right and 20° to the left); a firing range of 20° in depression and 20° in elevation, relative to the horizontal carriage. Other types of armament were tested and loaded such as the Swiss Solothurn heavy machine gun and others.

Engine: it was mounted transversely at the rear. It consisted of four vertical, single-block, four-stroke cylinders and developed a power of 43 HP at normal speed, energy was transmitted to two drive wheels. It was started by hand, by means of a crank, either from outside or inside the tank. The engine guaranteed a maximum speed of 42 km/h with an operating range of about 125 km.

Transmission organs: consisting of the drive shaft, clutch, gearbox and steering mechanism. The propeller shaft connects the engine shaft with the clutch and transmits motion to the gearbox and then to the steering mechanism.

The gearbox can provide four speeds for forward and one for reverse and, through the reduction gear, a second set of reduced speeds (four for forward and one for reverse).

Locomotive parts: consisting of drive wheels, idlers, track chains, track support beam, auxiliary rollers, bogies with load-bearing rollers.

The driving wheels, made of steel, are located at the front of the tank, one on each side. Each wheel consists of a toothed disc (15 teeth) on which the tracks engage.

The deflection wheels are made of bronze, located at the rear of the tank (one on each side); they turn in neutral on a pin and they are connected to the auxiliary rollers. The action of a sleeve makes it possible to vary the position of the pin of the idler wheel and thus increase or decrease the tension of the track.

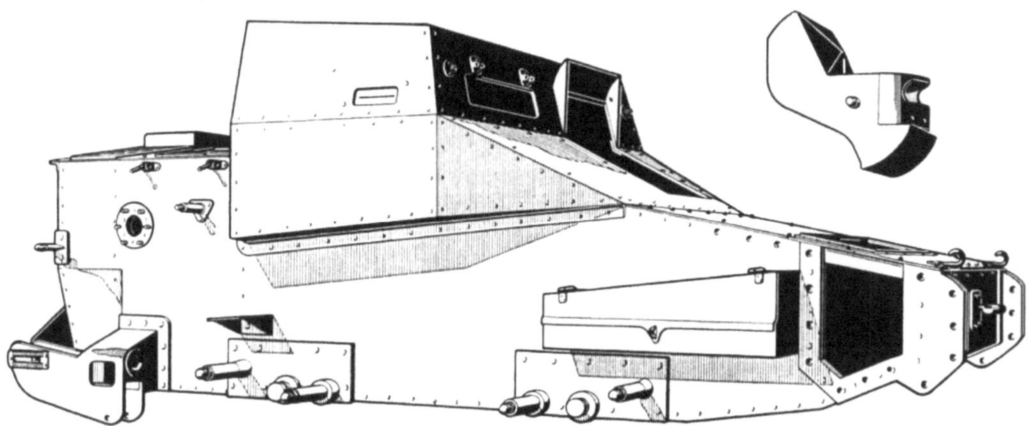

▲ Drawing of CV 33 series 1 body, made of metal sheet assembled by riveting and brazing.

The tracks, two in number, one on each side, are composed of 72 main and 72 auxiliary links, of pressed steel, connected by pins and plates. Each main link has a window –into which the drive wheel teeth penetrate– and two fins that serve to guide the load-bearing rollers and prevent slipping. Each main link also has two ribs for gripping the track to the ground and, on the side, three perforated appendages for the passage of the connecting pin. The auxiliary links are devoid of the outer ribs and window.

The acacia-wood, trapezoidal-section track-bearing spars, designed to support the track above, are also two and arranged on the sides of the tank.

The load-bearing bogies constitute, together with leaf springs, the suspension of the tank and there are two per side, connected by spars rigidly attached to the sides of the tank. Each bogie is equipped with three rubberised, load-bearing rollers. The bogies distribute the weight of the tank sufficiently evenly over the load-bearing rollers; they also allow elastic suspension of the hull and enable the track to adapt to uneven terrain.

▼ CV 3-05, 4-cylinder in-line gasoline engine.

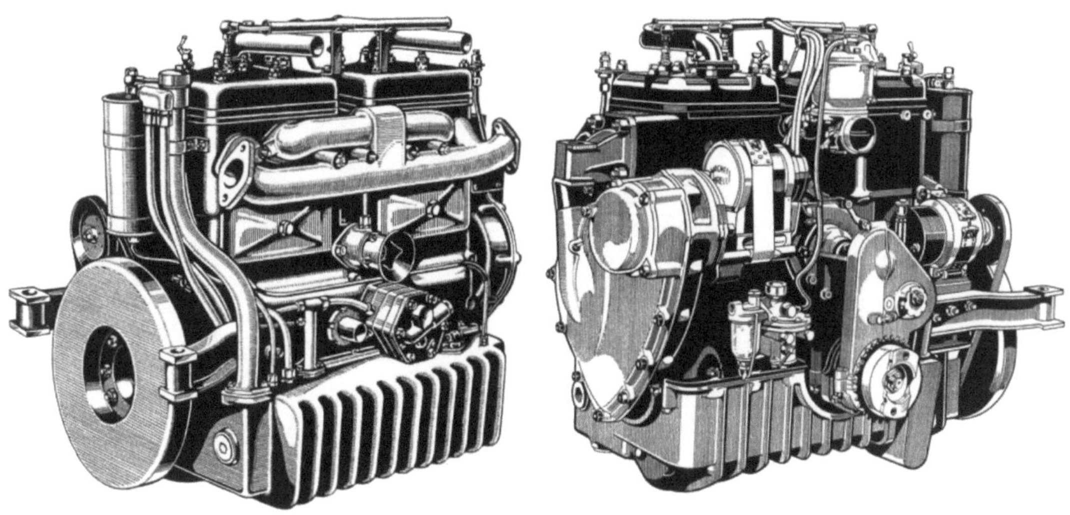

Control elements: these are operated by two control or direction levers. Located inside the hull, to the right and left of the driver, they each control two steering mechanism locking blocks; a brake pedal intensifies the block locking action and a clutch pedal and levers control the clutch. The levers, pedals and shackles, acting under the action of the driver, allow straight travel, right and left rotation and stopping of the tank. The rotation of the tank is obtained by slowing down or stopping the motion of one of the tracks through the action of the control or direction levers (the tank rotates on the side from which the braking or locking of the track has occurred); stopping is obtained following the simultaneous locking of the two, tracks.

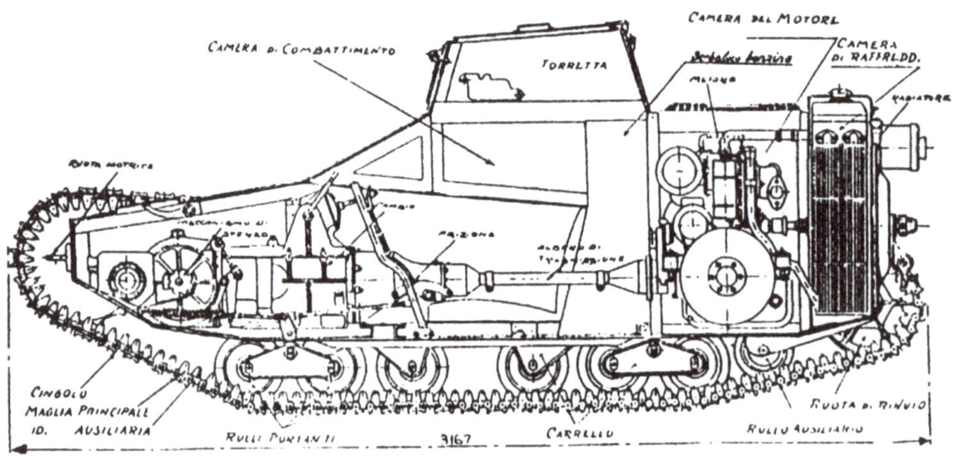

▲ Drawing from the original manual of the Longitudinal Section of a CV 33 Series 1.

▼ Fossati factory, Genoa - Sestri Ponente, light tank production sector.

ITALIAN LIGHT TANKS L3/33-35-38

VEHICLE VERSIONS

Numerous versions of the light fast tank were produced, including definitive operatives and prototypes, the most important of which are listed below.

• *CV33 1st Series*: first designation of Ansaldo's fast tank, armed with a Fiat 14 cal. 6.5 mm aviation machine gun. All 1st Series tanks were later rearmed by a gun of the same type, adapted to 8 mm calibre.

• *CV33 2nd Series (Mod.34)*: appearing in 1934 but distributed in 1936, this version introduced the twin 8 mm FIAT Mod.14 machine gun and the separation of the tensioning wheel from the rear wheel. The hinges of the pilot hatch are inside the body, the replacement of the rear doors with hatches, the ventilation door protected by a metal plate and other changes to the external fittings complete the version. In 1938, these copies were renamed L3 / 33 then L33 in 1940.

• *CV35 1st Series*: variant of the previous series. The differences are reduced to a few welded rather than riveted body plates. The initial guns were replaced by FIAT Mod.35 or Breda Mod.38 machine guns. In 1938, this series was renamed L3 / 35 then L35 in 1940.

• *CV35 2nd Series*: almost the same as the previous one, with minor modifications in terms of details and embrasures.

• *CV30 or L3/38*: this series was tested in 1937. The prototype had a new gear, with an enlarged diameter for the four bogie wheels and a new suspension. The two 8 mm machine guns were replaced by Breda Mod.31 Type Marina 13.2 mm models. From 1940 this model was called the L38.

• *L3 lf (C.V. Flamethrower)*: its development began in 1935. It mounted a flame thrower tube in the place of one of the machine guns, which was fed by an external tank that could be either mounted on the engine inspection hatch or on a special trailer. The modification was carried out on both C.V.33 and C.V.35 hulls. The vehicle therefore weighed 5 tonnes. This vehicle was used in Abyssinia, Spain, France, the Balkans, North Africa and Italian East Africa.

• *L3/r (C.V. With radio equipment)*: equipped with a radio and used as a command tank, intended for squadron (or company) or squadron group (or battalion) commanders.

• *L3 (Fast gangway tank)*: adapted for the transport and deployment of a gangway with a maximum length of 6/7 metres. Without armament. Prototype.

• *L3 (Recovery fast tank)*: equipped at the rear with a coupling system for recovering damaged or broken-down tanks. Prototype.

• *L3 (Solothurn fast tank)*: modification carried out on only a few examples directly at operational units in North Africa in 1941. Instead of twin machine guns it was equipped with a Swiss Solothurn S-18/1000 20 mm anti-tank gun.

• *L35 Airborne*: flamethrower version of the L3/35, suitable for airborne transport.

• *CV33 Training*: from 1941 some units, withdrawn from the front line as obsolete, and deprived of armament were used for tank training.

• *Trubia*: experimental version designed for nationalist Spain, armed with a 20 mm Breda Mod.35 cannon.

• *L3 light tractor*: version designed as a light tractor for a 47/32 mm cannon.

• *L3 demolition tractor*: a unique radio-controlled prototype intended for the destruction of minefields or fortifications, an idea similar to the German Goliath.

• *L3 47/32 self-propelled gun*: only two prototypes of this open-hulled self-propelled gun were made, one by Fiat and the other by Breda. Vehicle equipped with a 47 mm anti-tank gun.

■ LIGHT TANK CV 33

The tests of the four pre-series examples carried out in Sciarborasca (province of Genoa) were successfully concluded in July 1933, and the inclined tank was entered in the army inventory under the name Carro Veloce Ansaldo (Fast Tanks Arnaldo). A first order for 240 examples of the CV33 was placed in 1933. With the arrival of General Baistrocchi as the new undersecretary of war, a new order for 500 examples was placed in 1934. By the spring of 1935, the CV33s had been distributed to the three groups of the fast divisions (138 examples), to a company in Bologna (15 examples) and to a unit in Somalia (30 examples). The CV33

▶▼ CV33 tanks crossing a bridge.

Middle: detail of the twin-arm of a CV35.

Below: CV 33 tanks in training before the war. (P. Crippa Archives)

underwent some modifications compared to the pre-production models: the air intakes were replaced by less vulnerable 14 x 6 cm parts, the headlights were moved into the cockpit and the toolboxes returned to their original position behind the cogwheel (they were located behind the cockpit, on either side of the engine compartment, in the pre-production models).

The Italian vehicle was compact, to say the least: its dimensions were close to those of the Fiat Topolino. The body was made of steel plates assembled by riveting and brazing in the passenger compartment. The armour, between 6 mm (rear) and 14 mm (passenger compartment) thick, only offered protection against bullets from enemy rifles and machine guns.

Two transverse partitions divide the body into three parts: the cockpit or combat compartment at the front, the engine and the so-called cooling compartment where the radiator is located. In the cockpit, where the tank commander (left seat) and the pilot (right seat) sit, are the weapons and fuel tank. The cockpit roof is open and has two hatches for crew access.

The CV 33 is powered by an inline four-cylinder engine developing 43 hp.

The gearing consists of a 15-tooth steel pinion at the front, a bronze tension wheel at the rear preceded by a guide roller, both partially covered by the same plate, and two carriages with three rollers each.

The 6.5 mm Fiat mod.14 machine gun has a 40° sector of fire (20° to the right and left) and a 30° angle of fire (12° in depression and 18° in elevation). It is equipped with 3,800 rounds. Metal magazines of 50 or 100 rounds are stored in six wooden boxes.

The CV 33 Series 2, which appeared in 1934, was armed with twin Fiat Model 14/35 8 mm machine guns. Other details that differentiated it from the Series 1 were the removal of the air

▼ CV33 Light tanks during military maneuvers in the second half of the 1930s.(Archive P. Crippa)

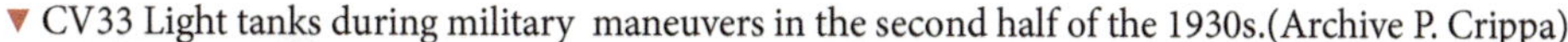

intakes on the rear wall of the cockpit and the separation of the guide roller and tensioning wheel mounts. From 1935 onwards, many CV 33 Series 1s were fitted with twin Fiat Model 14/35 machine guns.

LIGHT TANK CV 35

In 1935, based on engine No. 798, a new version of the light tank appeared on the assembly lines: the CV35 series 1, which began to be distributed to units in the first half of 1936. It differed from the CV33 in that its casemate was entirely riveted instead of welded. On the CV35 series 2 (from engine no. 1341), the side doors were protected by bolted reinforcements. At the same time, the shape of the rear of the cockpit, broken at the ends, became straight, which simplified the manufacturing process. From 1939, the Fiat mod.14/35 machine guns were replaced by the Breda mod.38, also 8 mm. The gun was equipped with 1,896 rounds and could carry 79 magazines of 24 rounds.

LIGHT TANK CV 38

The last version of the Italian tracked tank, the CV38, was tested in 1937 during large-scale manoeuvres in Sicily, more precisely in Erice (province of Trapani). The prototype with the registration number RE 2286 was obtained from a CV35 with a fully converted gear. It consisted of two bogies on each side with two larger diameter rollers, suspended by torsion bars. Its armament was limited to a Breda mod.31 13.2 mm *marine type* machine gun.

To test the new undercarriage, several tracked vehicles were modified and tested in

▲ An L3/38 stopped at an Italian checkpoint in Karlovac, now a Croatian town, on April 5, 1942 (Archive P. Crippa)

▼ CV35 tank moving over impervious terrain (P. Crippa Archive).

▲ The small CV33 was suitable for being photographed by tankers who posed above the vehicle (Author archive).

▼ Model of CV33 RFCA 37 Radio. Made by Model Victoria (www.modelvictoria.it).

▲ CV33 flamethrowers in action (P. Crippa Archives).

▼ Another CV33 flamethrower version tank with armor painted sand yellow (P. Crippa Archives).

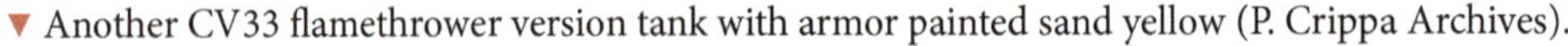

▲ Motorized artillery and light tanks CV33 (command version with radio) in Val Stretta (Bardonecchia) in June 1940. Concession State Archives. Photo colored by the author.

units. But it was not until June 1941 that a 'large-scale' conversion programme was established: it was to cover at least 160 L3s. In 1942, only 52 units benefited, and a further 32 between January and July 1943. In the end, only two battalions could be uniformly equipped with L38s. The modified tanks retained their original armament. The toolboxes were moved behind the cockpit on both sides of the engine compartment.

◼ RADIO TANKS

As the basic vehicles lacked any means of radio communication, a set derived from the R3 was installed in 1934 on an experimental basis against the left side of the cockpit of a CV33 of the first series. The semi-circular antenna was mounted on the roof of the left cockpit and at the rear end of the body. The batteries were housed in two boxes attached to the rear of the cockpit in place of the spare rollers, which were placed on the lid of these boxes.

The R3 CV radio was fitted from 1935 onwards to the tanks of battalion and company commanders of the CV33 series 2 that took part in the Ethiopian campaign. Its theoretical range was between 5 and 8 km when the vehicle was stationary, depending on the nature of the terrain. With the tank in motion, the range did not exceed 2 km.

The radio version of the CV 35 was similar to that based on the CV 33. Proportionally, fewer CV 35s were converted into radio tanks than on the CV 33. On some examples, the guns were removed to make more room in the cockpit of the command/radio tank.

A more unusual version appeared on the CV 35, featuring a German Siemens ultra-short-wave radio combined with a large, 2 metre-high flexible antenna fixed to the front of the cockpit. Two such equipped tanks were tested by the 8th *Battalion* from January 1939 and took part in important manoeuvres in Piedmont in the summer. But this version did not give the expected satisfaction and the experiment stopped there.

Since 1940, the R3 CV radios were gradually replaced by the RF 1 CA with a telescopic antenna mounted on the rear of the cockpit and then on the right battery box.

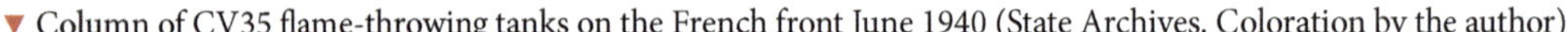

▼ Column of CV35 flame-throwing tanks on the French front June 1940 (State Archives. Coloration by the author).

■ FLAMETHROWER TANKS

Various flame-thrower versions were developed on the basis of the CV33 and its successors. The prototype was built on a CV33 series 1 by the Fiat-OCI company in Modena in 1935 and sent to Rome for evaluation. Adopted in August 1935, the CV33 Lf was produced on the basis of CV33 series 2 and then CV35s sent directly from the Ansaldo factory to Fiat-OCI, which equipped them.

As space on board the CV33 was very limited, the flammable liquid (60% engine oil and 40% fuel oil) was transported in a 520-litre tank trailer. The tank trailer had a reinforcement of between 6 and 8.5 mm and an empty weight of 830 kg. The liquid was conveyed into the tank by a canvas tube lined and protected by steel rings to prevent it from breaking. A pump connected to the engine brought the liquid to a pressure of 7-10 bar. Each use of the flamethrower absorbed 5 hp of engine power. The ignition liquid (a mixture of oil and petrol) was contained in a 10-litre tank located against the left bulkhead of the cockpit. The firing system consisted of the flammable liquid tube, the ignition liquid tube and the electrical contact wire. The practical operational range was about 60 m. The first engagements of the CV33 and 35 Lf in Ethiopia proved that the use of the trailer was inappropriate because it was too vulnerable and too heavy. In addition, the trailer arm proved too fragile, forcing the crews to fill the tank only half full. As a temporary remedy, at least three tanks deployed in Somalia mounted a horizontal cylindrical fuel barrel on the engine cover. In Spain, a 306-litre tank, also mounted on the bonnet, was used, a trick that proved to be an effective and safe solution.

The last attempt to modify the flamethrower tank was the installation of a 135-litre prismatic armoured tank on the engine cover. This was approved because the new tank was not too visible a target. A small series of 10 tanks was built to form a transportable air company within the *4th Tank Regiment* in Rome. The lack of Savoia Marchetti S.82s, the only aircraft capable of transporting them, caused the project to fail in October 1941. The tanks were therefore transferred to other units.

The L3 flamethrower version with trailer remained the standard for the Italian army until 1943. In the early autumn of 1941, there were still about 100 of these tanks in the units.

▼ 47/32 Self-propelled L3 version (author's coloration).

■ FINAL NOTES ON NAMES

It is now appropriate to review the various names of the Ansaldo tank. In June 1938, CV33, 35 and 35 were renamed L33, 35 and 38. Then, in June 1940, their names became L3/33, L3/35 and L3/38, with the weight indicated in front of the year of production (in theory, since we have seen that the conversion of the L38 did not really begin until 1941). Finally, after August 1942, the designations L33, 35 and 38 were re-established.

► Exercise of the walkway tank (Archive P. Crippa)

► Exercise of the walkway tank under the watchful eyes of staff officers. (P. Crippa archive).

▼ CV33 2nd series of the Pinerolo Cavalry School in March 1938. The machine guns have been removed (Giacomo Corda archive)

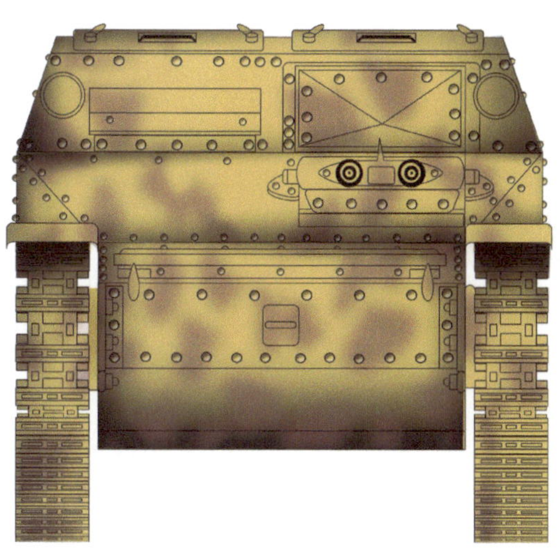

▲ ▼ ► three views of a CV 35 profile. Author artwork

WW2 ITALIAN TANK &AFV COLORS & CAMOUFLAGE

light green
1936-1943 camouflage

Italian green gray
1936-1945

reddish brown
1936-1943

light yellow sand
1941-1945

dark yellow sand
1943-1945

variant yellow sand
1941-1945

dark green
1936-1943 camouflage

gun metal-gingers

deep rubber

panzer grey
1943-1945

Italian tankers veste

khaki north Afrika

Italian minio red

internal Italian white

▲ CV33 2nd series of the Guide cavalry regiment in Ethiopia, with IMAM Ro 1 in the background (Aymeric Lopez Archives).

▼ L3/33 flamethrower displayed in the museum in Bovington UK (Wikipedia).

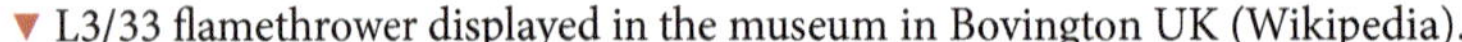

OPERATIONAL USE

Starting in 1933, the year of its entry into service, CV33 was present in all wartime events involving Italy until 1945.

⬛ FIRST DEPLOYMENT IN SAARLAND AND BAPTISM OF FIRE IN ETHIOPIA

The first unit to handle the new machine was the *19th Guide Cavalry Regiment* in the summer of 1934. The *3rd squadron* of this regiment (consisting of 13 tanks) took part in the international election control mission in the Saarland (German territory bordering Luxembourg and Lorraine) between December 1934 and January 1935.

The 10 CV33s sent to Somalia in February 1934 had their baptism of fire during the Ethiopian attack on Ual Ual in the Ogaden on 5 December 1934, which served as a casus belli for the conquest of Ethiopia between October 1935 and May 1936. The Italian army sent 112 L3s to Eritrea and 45 to Somalia before the start of hostilities, and more followed during the course of the conflict, to reach a total of almost 250. On the northern front, two tank squadrons were formed, while on the southern front, considered at the beginning of the campaign as secondary, only the *1st Somalia Tank Battalion* was initially deployed, with two companies. It was later joined by the *20th Randaccio Battalion* with 46 L3, to which 12 flame-throwing tanks and 3 radio tanks were added in December 1935. In mid-March 1936, the two units were merged into the *Somalia Tank Grouping*, in two groups of three companies each. The southern front soon proved to be the most suitable for tank action due to its vast plains, while the mountainous terrain of northern Ethiopia was a major handicap to their action. However, this war experience demonstrated their good manoeuvrability in difficult terrain. Several L3s were lost during this campaign: once immobilised, the tank was easy prey for Ethiopian soldiers, as only the front sector of the tank was defended. Moreover, to get out of the tank, the crew had to expose themselves to enemy fire.

▼ CV33 1st series of the 3rd squadron of the 19th Guide regiment in Saarland, winter of 1934-1935 (A. Lopez archive).

■ L3 TANKS IN THE SPANISH WAR

The first five CV35s landed in Vigo (Galicia) on 27 August 1936 and, together with the next ten that arrived on 29 September in the same port, formed the first mixed Italian-Spanish unit formally attached to the Spanish Foreign Legion, the *Tercio*. This unit fought in the vicinity of Madrid before being disbanded. Two companies of L3 were then sent to Spain in November 1936 and January 1937, and a full battalion was embarked on 31 January 1937, landing in Spain on 6 February. Its arrival enabled the formation of the *Assault Tank and Armoured Car Grouping* of 5 tank companies and 1 squadron of 8 self-propelled guns on 17 February. The unit changed its name on 22 February to *Raggruppamento Reparti Specialializzati*, then commanded by Colonel Carlo Rivolta, and supplemented by a motorized gun company and, from 6 March, a flamethrower company.

After participating in the battles of Malaga and Guadalajara in February and March 1937, the *Specialised Units Regiment* was reorganised into two battalions. Colonel Valentino Babini took command of the unit on 25 April 1937. In August 1937, the *Specialised Regiment* took part in the Battle of Santander before being renamed the *Tank Regiment* on 25 September. This unit then participated in the Battles of Aragon between March and April 1938, of Ebro between July and November 1938 and of Catalonia between December 1938 and March 1939.

A total of 157 L3 tracked vehicles were sent to Spain. At the end of the Civil War, some of the surviving vehicles were handed over to the Nationalist troops.

This campaign was the first opportunity for the Italian tracked vehicles to face real tanks: the Russian T-26 and BT-5 armed with 45 mm cannons, which were used by the Republican troops. As the L3s' machine guns were totally ineffective against these tanks, the Italian L3s sometimes towed German 37 mm anti-tank guns, which came into action when necessary. Despite this, Italian losses were light: a dozen L3s were destroyed between November 1936 and January 1939, including three flamethrowers, and five were captured. It must be said that Soviet tanks were often used rationally and, despite their superiority in terms of armament and protection, the T-26s were too slow and prone to frequent breakdowns.

■ ALBANIAN CAMPAIGN

In April 1939, the 134 L3s of the 31st *Tank Regiment* of the *Centaur Division*, the 63s of the 3rd *Fast Tank Group San Giorgio* and a few others from the *2nd Bersaglieri Regiment* took part in the occupation of Albania. But this operation was practically only a kind of extensive exercise, as there was hardly any fighting. However, the operation revealed great disorganisation within the Army: the tanks could not disembark at the scheduled time due to congestion in the port of Vlora, and once ashore, it was realised that fuel supplies were non-existent... Unfortunately, no lessons were learned.

■ L3 TANKS ON ALL FRONTS IN THE SECOND WORLD WAR

On the eve of the war in 1939, Italy organised three armoured divisions: the *132nd Armoured Division Ariete* in February, the *131st Armoured Division Centauro* in April and the *133rd Armoured Division Littorio* in October. Each of these comprised one armoured regiment out of four L3 battalions, with a theoretical strength of 184 tanks, a bersaglieri regiment and a motorised artillery regiment. On 10 June 1940, the tanks still equipped 10 battalions of the three armoured divisions, eight independent battalions in metropolitan France, six battalions in Libya, three fast cavalry tank groups, a mixed battalion in Rhodes (on L3s and Fiat 3000s), a mechanised company in Zara and a cavalry squadron in East Africa. These units amounted to 800 L3s in mainland France (of which 211 were in reserve and 112 used for training), 130 in Albania with the *Centaur*, almost 300 in Libya and 15 in East Africa.

LIGHT TANKS IN THE ETHIOPIAN WAR 1935-1936

▲ L3/33 of the "Guide" cavalry regiment in Ethiopia. The tank badges of the vehicles assigned to the cavalry were of the three types: cavalry, light cavalry and lancers. The Guide was marked with the color light blue. This color was also used for the name of the tank. This image is taken from a photo in this book on page 20. The camouflage of the tanks sent to Ethiopia was with reddish-brown background color with thick camouflage in green or gray green.

▲ CV33 on parade in Piazza della Vittoria in Genoa, around 1937 (author's coloration).

▼ CV35 R stored in the Military Museum of South Africa. (Courtesy Wikipedia)

LIGHT TANKS IN THE ETHIOPIAN WAR 1935-1936

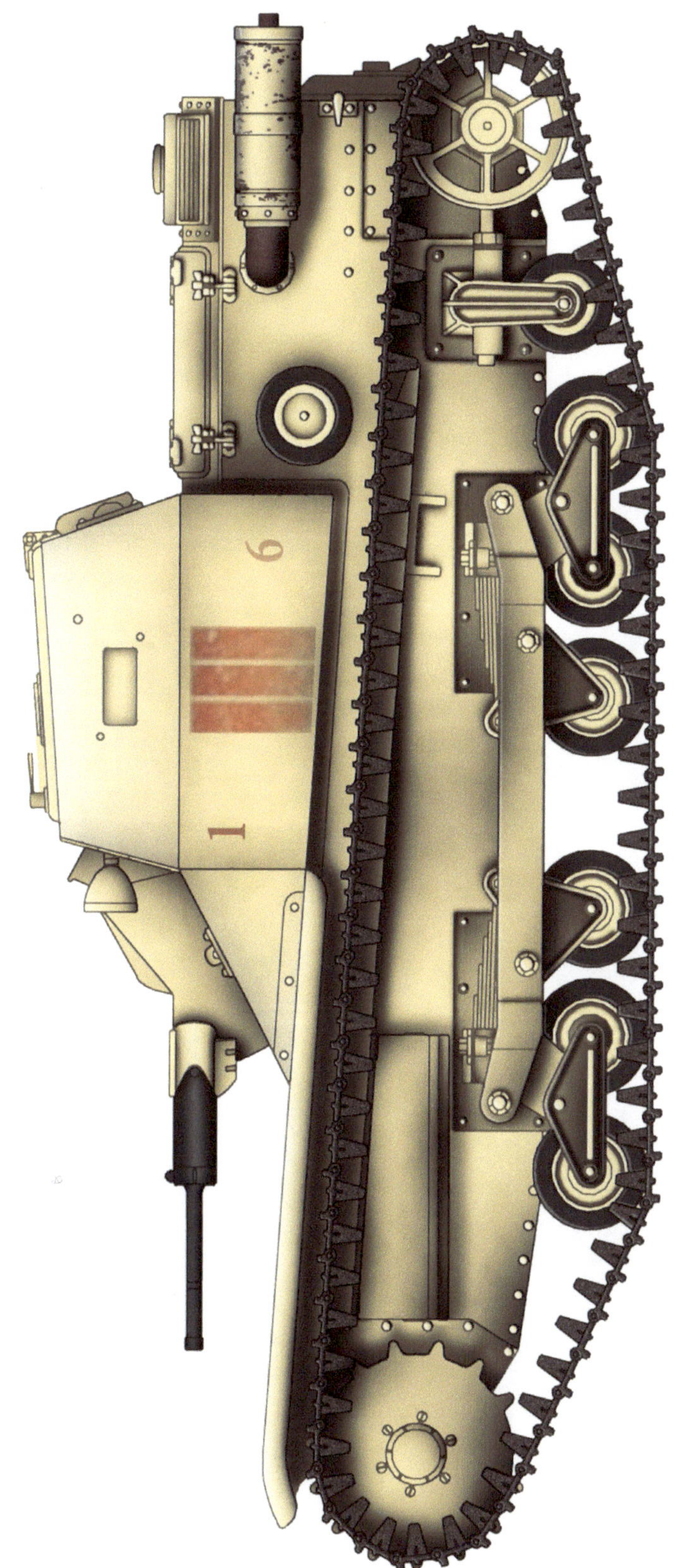

▲ L3/33 2nd series in force at the southern front in Somalia. This specific tank was commanded by Staff Sergeant Rosolino Sarotti of the tank command in Somalia in 1936. Light sand color. Red stripes indicate: 1st Company (red) of 3rd Platoon (three stripes).

▶ CV33 F advancing toward Malaga in February 1937 (Aymeric Lopez Archive).

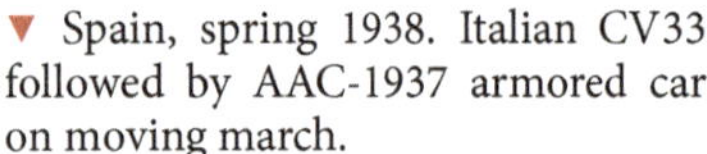

▼ Spain, spring 1938. Italian CV33 followed by AAC-1937 armored car on moving march.

The first L3 unit to be engaged in operations at the beginning of World War II was the *33rd Tank Regiment* of the *Littorio Division*, under the command of Colonel De Lorenzis. Transferred to the Aosta Valley on 19 June 1940, the regiment had four L3 battalions. At dawn on 23 June, the *1st battalion* received orders to march towards the village of Séez, via the Petit Saint-Bernard pass. But the column ran into a minefield that destroyed the first tank, while the others managed to turn back under French artillery fire. Another tank was lost under the same circumstances on the evening of 23 June while trying to recover the one that had been lost in the morning. On 24 June, at the Mont-Cenis pass, the *1st Company* of the *4th Battalion* of the *1st Tank Infantry Regiment* managed to descend into Val d'Arc, although the commander's tank was blown up by a mine and a second was damaged. These actions, conducted without preparation or artillery support, demonstrated the inadequacy of tracked vehicles to fight against fortified works, even without anti-tank guns.

THE CAMPAIGN IN GREECE

On 28 October 1940, when war was declared against Greece, the *31st Centauro Regiment*, stationed in Albania since April 1939, attacked the Drin and Vjosa (Vojussa in Italian) valleys in the direction of Kalibaki and Ioannina (Giannina in Italian). At the time, the unit had four L tank battalions, with a total of 170 tracked tanks, 37 of which were flame throwers. Major fighting took place towards Kalibaki, with the loss of 14 tanks. The mud made tank manoeuvres very difficult, and the crossing of the Vjosa was complicated by the destruction of the bridges by the Greeks. During the Italian retreat, the L3s acted as a rearguard to slow down the Greek counter-offensive. In January 1941, the *2nd L tank battalion* and the *4th M tank* operated between Tepelen (Tepeleni in Italian) and Klisura, along the Vjosa. At the end of March, the regiment was redeployed to Tirana with the remaining 50 light tanks and 15 M13/40 before being directed (with the exception of the *3rd* battalion) to the Albanian-Yugoslav border on April 4.

▼ CV33 captured by the Greeks and later abandoned in the countryside (Italian State Archives).

THE CAMPAIGN IN YUGOSLAVIA

In the north, the *33rd Littorio Regiment*, with three tank battalions totalling 117 L3, was put on alert at the Italian-Yugoslav border at the end of March 1941. On the night of 10-11 April, the L3s of this division left Rijeka along the Dalmatian coast towards Mostar, more than 1,000 km away, almost without encountering resistance. On the southern front, however, in the area of Lake Shkodra, the Italian troops initially remained on the defensive. The *31st regiment* defended the Koplik sector, repelling Yugoslav attacks. Finally, on 15 April, the regiment advanced towards the Yugoslav border with orders not to open fire beforehand due to the ongoing armistice negotiations. But the Yugoslavs were ready for the Italian tanks: 11 L3s were lost and five others damaged. Despite this difficult start, the *Centauro* entered Yugoslav territory the next day and crossed into Montenegro. The columns of the two Italian armoured divisions met on 18 April, between Trebinje and Dubrovnik (Ragusa in Italian). The two regiments returned to Italy in May and June 1941.

LANDING IN CRETE

A company of 13 L3s manning the *CCCXII mixed battalion* was deployed in a small landing operation on Crete on 28 May 1941. The battalion then remained in service on the island of Rhodes, passing to the side of the RSI in September 1943.

THE WAR IN AFRICA

In the AOI, Italian troops had 39 L3 tracked vehicles at their disposal on 15 July 1940, thanks to reinforcements from the *3rd Bologna Regiment*. On 4 July 1940, two platoons of the *1st Special Tank Company* L participated in the capture of Kassala, on the Sudanese border, together with 12 M11/39s. In August, 15 L3 of the Knights of Neghelli fast tank squadron took part in the invasion of British Somalia. Subsequently, all these vehicles were lost during the defence of the

▼ Tank of the *6th Company* of the *3rd Battalion* of the *31st Infantrymen Regiment* in Montenegro after September 8, 1943. The unit, upon news of the Armistice, decided to continue fighting alongside the Germans (Bundesarchiv).

▲ 1937-38 Sixth L3/33 tank of the 1st company of the "Italian-Spanish Tank and Artillery Grouping" of the Italian CTV corps. The first five light tanks were sent from Italy to Vigo to aid Spanish nationalist forces. By the end of the war there will be about a hundred vehicles used in the course of the conflict.

▲ Fiat-Ansaldo CV33/35 rearmed with 20mm Breda M-35s. Experimental conversion made in 1937 during the Spanish Civil War (an attempt due to the intent to provide the Nationalist tanks with a stronger weapon to counter the Soviet tanks supplied to the Republicans). Only two units were made.

empire, either to enemy fire or due to a lack of spare parts.

In June 1940, the L3 was the only Italian 'tank' present in Cyrenaica, manning six battalions (the *IX, XX, XXI, LX, LXI* and *LXII*), plus the *LXIII* that arrived at the end of the month. On the night of 15 to 16 June, the first battle took place between the L3s of two companies of the *9th battalion* and British armoured troops in the Sidi Omar area. The Italian column was blown to pieces despite the bravery of the crews, demonstrating the impotence of the crawlers against modern armoured vehicles.

In preparation for the offensive on Sidi Barrani, the tracked units were nominally combined into two tank groupings at the end of August, each comprising three L tank battalions and one M 11/39. But in practice, the battalions continued to operate separately from each other. Only the *Maletti Grouping*, with a company of the *LXI Tank Battalion* in its ranks, fought with several armoured and motorised units. On 25 November 1940, the *Special Armoured Brigade* under the command of General Babini was created in the Marsa Lugh sector. It comprised the *XXI* and *LXI L-battalions* with 152 tanks, but was not fully operational. The *LXI battalion*, detached from the *Maletti group*, came under the command of the *1st CC.NN division 23 March* in December. During the Wavell counter-offensive, launched on 9 December 1940, all 7 L tank battalions were destroyed or captured. The British captured 116 L3s during the capture of Bardia on 4 January 1941, but few of them were still operational. By the end of the counter-offensive, the British army had recovered 45 combat-capable armoured vehicles.

In January and February 1941, to partially replace these losses, the *5th Battalion* mobilised in the *3rd Regiment* and assigned to the Pavia Division, as well as the *32nd Aries Regiment* with three L-tank battalions with 117 L3s, of which 24 flamethrowers had just landed, participated in the reconquest of Cyrenaica with the *5th Leichte Division*. In April 1941, the L3s were launched against the defences of Tobruk to no avail. With the formation of the *132nd Regiment* equipped with M 13/40s, the L3s became secondary. The *3rd L tank battalion* of the *32nd regiment* was assigned to RECAM when it was formed in November 1941. But the L3s could not be used to counter Operation Crusader, and the *32nd Regiment* was repatriated on 8 January 1942. An official report of May 1942 still mentions the presence of 22 L3s in North Africa, relegated to secondary duties.

■ RUSSIAN CAMPAIGN

On the Russian front, tracked vehicles made their appearance as part of the *3rd San Giorgio* fast tank group, attached to the *3rd Principe Amedeo Duca d'Aosta Celere Division* from August 1941. But the group, divided into four squadrons, encountered serious logistical and climatic difficulties that caused several vehicles to be abandoned. By January 1942, the group no longer had any operational L3s, and was therefore repatriated in July 1942.

■ LAST OPERATIONS IN DALMATIA, FRANCE AND SICILY

In the Balkans, L3 action was not limited to operations in Greece and Yugoslavia. Already in July 1941, the *1st* and *2nd L battalions* of the *31st Tank Regiment* were sent to Dalmatia to fight partisan action, before being replaced at the end of September by the *3rd battalion* of the same regiment. In November 1941, the *1st Flamethrower Battalion* was formed out of 37 L3 and sent to Yugoslavia. At the end of March 1942, the *2nd Flamethrower Tank Battalion* of the *4th Regiment*, reduced to 16 L3s, was sent to Montenegro, where it operated for a year. At the same time, the 12 L 3/35 flamethrowers of the *2nd Autonomous Company* were deployed to Slovenia and Dalmatia. SUPERSLODA also had the *1st L San Giusto tank group* in Split with 45 L3s and the *2nd L San Marco* tank group in Dalmatia with 30 vehicles. Thus, in the first half of 1942, out of a total of 373 operational L3 tanks, 191 were deployed in the Balkans. In the late summer of 1942, the *31st Regiment* formed an autonomous company that was sent to Montenegro.

In November 1942, during the Italian occupation of southern France, L3s from the *2nd San Marco Group* and the *3rd Piedmont Royal Squadron* were sent to the French Riviera. The *13th L tank battalion* of the *32nd regiment* and the *1st battalion* of the *33rd regiment*, based in Sardinia, were sent to Corsica with around 70 L3s. After the armistice, this unit participated in the liberation of the island by fighting the German troops.

Incredible as it may seem, some 30 L3s from the *12th battalion* of the *4th regiment* based in Sicily were deployed in the defence of the island in July 1943. By the time of the armistice on 8 September 1943, 638 L3s remained in the Regio Esercito. By then, losses amounted to 689 tracked vehicles, of which 458 were in North Africa.

L3 TANKS AFTER THE ARMISTICE

After the armistice of 8 September 1943, only one L3 battalion of the 11 still existing ones sided with the Germans. The Germans, however, rounded up a large number of vehicles, reusing them mainly in the Balkans. Some 40 L3s were used by the armoured units of the RSI, particularly the *Leonessa* (which had 16 in all versions), *Leoncello* and *San Giusto* armoured groups, the Anti-Partisan Regiment as well as the *Tagliamento Assault Legion* and the *Ettore Mutti Mobile Autonomous Legion*. These participated in the fighting against partisan forces in northern Italy until April 1945. Some L3 were also captured by the Partisans in Italy and Yugoslavia.

▼ A CV35 of the Littorio Division on the French front in June 1940. (State Archives. Author's coloration).

L3 FAST TANKS FLAMETHROWER VERSION

▲ CV33/35 flamethrower version. The flamethrower carriage along with the gangway carriage were certainly the most curious versions of the entire L3 project. The flamethrower was later refined in turn into other solutions, all of which were aimed at avoiding the dependence on the towed undercarriage that had proved to be something of an Achilles' heel.

▲ A CV35 of the Littorio among soldiers on the French front in June 1940 (State Archives. Author's coloration).

▼ A Greek soldier sitting on the hull of an abandoned L3 tank during the Italians' retreat from Epirus.

FAST TANKS IN THE WAR IN AFRICA 1940-1943

▲ 1941 Second Tank, 2nd Company, 3rd Platoon L3/35 of the 132nd Aries Armored Division in Libya. This plate reproduces the tank preserved at the Canadian War Museum in Ottawa, Canada, which has some errors in the coloring, the most obvious of which is the presence of the Aries Division shield on the casemate.

▲ L33 Radio of the IX Battalion of the 102nd Motorized Division "Trento" in Libya, December 1941. The radio tank was equipped with the new Swiss Solothurn anti-tank gun.

▲ L3/33 2nd series in North Africa (Courtesy of Aymeric Lopez).

▼ CV33 flamethrower at the Bovington Museum. Note the distinctive mark on the back of the vehicle (Wikipedia).

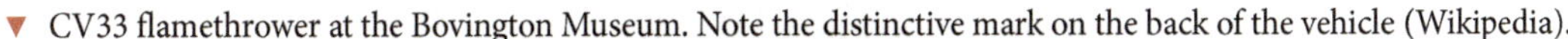

▲ L35 in snow camouflage outfit belonging to ARMIR Groups Stalino area November 1942. Above left: bronze or aluminum badge that was placed on the upper left front plate of armored vehicles from April 1936 to August 1943.

CAMOUFLAGE AND DISTINGUISHED MARKS

The background colours of the light tanks from their creation until 1945, (the operational period of this use is indicated in brackets) also used for all armoured vehicles were: grey green R.E. (1936-1945), dark chocolate (1936-1941), reddish brown (1936-1943), ochre (for prototypes), sand (1941-1945), dark sand (1943-1945), dark grey (1941-1943). For camouflage, medium green (1936-1943) and dark red (for prototypes) were used.

The use of these colours in the various theatres of war was as follows: *Ethiopian War 1935-1936* - reddish brown colour with dense medium green flecks or directly with the background colour. *Spanish Civil War 1937-1939* - grey-green colour (predominantly) or reddish brown with dense medium green flecks. *National territory 1936-1940* - as in Spain again with a clear grey-green predominance. *Occupation of Albania and French Front 1939-1940* - grey-green.
Campaign of Greece and Yugoslavia 1940-1941 - camouflaged grey-green with green and sand-coloured speckles. *East Africa 1940-1941* - grey-green or in the old Ethiopian campaign camouflage reddish brown with green spots. *North Africa 1940-1943* - at first only green-grey then sand-coloured in various variegated versions. *Russian Campaign 1941-1943* - grey green heavily camouflaged with mud, sand colour or bleached snow effect. *France and Corsica 1942* - grey green and sand with reddish brown patches. *CSR 1943-1945* - German dark sand colour, reddish brown with medium dense green flecks, in uniform German panzer grey colour. In particular, the tanks of the *Leonessa* and probably the *Leoncello* were dark sand in colour. Reddish brown camouflage those of the *San Giusto* and panzer grey-green those of the *Tagliamento*.

◼ FAST TANK BADGES

In order to recognise individual tanks in military operations, even for Italy, it became necessary to introduce an identification system, partly because there were no tanks with radio equipment installed. In fact, radios only began to be installed with some regularity in 1941. In the beginning, flags with red or white drapes were used for communication.

The first table of distinctive tank markings dates back to 1925 and was very complex and articulated to excess. Number groups were only introduced in 1927 after the establishment of the Tank Regiment, and new regulations were issued in 1928. In 1934, the first deliveries of CV33 finally began, which were distributed to the Tank Regiment until 1935 and the Cavalry Guide Regiment. The CV33s in use by the Tank Regiments bore the 'contoured' symbols on both sides. The numbers were painted on the front of the hull plate and on both sides.

The light tanks retained these symbols and this numbering until 1936, until the Tank Regiment was renamed in September and the first four Tank Infantry Regiments were born. In 1934, the Cavalry Guide Regiment was also transformed into the Fast Chariot Regiment. With the new regulations, the fast tanks of the groups and regiments were then identified by markings, names and numbers placed on the sides of the hull. In 1938, in order to simplify recognition, a further change was made, this time a radical one: new tactical symbols were established for the tanks.

The tank companies were represented by coloured rectangles as follows:

The first company had the colour red, the 2nd company blue, the 3rd company yellow, the 4th company green; the colour white was reserved for the command tanks. The insignia of the tanks and armoured cars had to be 20 x 12 cm in size and painted in the colour of the company.

The coloured rectangles were cut by white bars to indicate the different platoons, black for the command tanks. The rectangles of the tanks of the various platoons were surmounted by an Arabic number (of the company colour) indicating the tank in the organic formation of the platoon. These numbers had to be 10 cm high and 1.5 cm thick and placed in the centre of the upper side of the rectangle at a distance of 2 cm.

All tanks bore, at the rear, the Arabic number of the battalion on the right and that of the regiment on the left, both painted white. Battalion tanks bore the battalion number (Roman) and the regimental number (Arabic); if in reserve at regimental level they bore only the relative Arabic number. Specifically for the L3 tanks, the distinguishing mark was placed: laterally, in the centre of the figure of the 'lower plates for turret side parts' and posteriorly, in the upper right corner of the rear armour of the vehicle with the base of the rectangle at the height of the towing hook. Roman and Arabic numbers of the battalion and regiment: of the battalion in the upper right corner, of the regiment in the upper left corner of the rear wall of the central casemate.

As a sign of aerial identification on the vehicles, a white Savoy cross was sometimes painted in the summer of 1940, placed, depending on the type of vehicle, on the turret or engine compartment ceiling. Starting in 1941, a white disc 70 cm in diameter was painted in place of the cross. The L3s of the cavalry had different markings and respectively bore the regimental frieze in this way: the commander's tank had the frieze surmounted by the crown, the platoon commanders' tanks the same frieze without the crown. The other tanks instead bore the assigned name painted in the regiment's distinctive colour, underlined by as many lines as the platoon to which they belonged. The distinctive colours were: Nizza Cavalry crimson, Genoa yellow, Lancieri di Novara white, Lancieri di Montebello green, Cavalry of Lodi red and black, Cavalry of Lucca black and white, Lancieri di V.E. yellow and black, Cavalry of Monferrato crimson and black, Cavalry of Alessandria orange and black the Guides blue and white. When the distinctive colours were two, the use of the second prevailed. The ornaments were respectively: the flame for the cavalry regiments, the crossed lances for the lancers and the cornet for the cavalrymen and guides.

▼ CV33 of the *3rd Battalion* of the *31st Tank Regiment* in Montenegro in 1943. After the Armistice the unit continued to fight alongside the Germans, and the unusual cross visible in the photograph was placed on the tanks as an identifying symbol (Crippa Archives).

▲ L35 of II Group L Tank Squadrons "San Marco", Dalmatia 1942.

L3/35 during the Russian campaign (State Archives. Author's coloration).

CV35 on duty in the TODT Organization with two German soldiers posing.

FAST TANKS IN THE ITALIAN CIVIL WAR 1943-1945

▲ June 1944: L3/33 of the 1st Company of the Armored Geruppo M "Leonessa" of the Republican National Guard in Turin.

▲ Montenegro, September 1943: L3/35 of the 6th Company of the 3rd Battalion of the 31st Carristi Regiment, commanded by Captain Ulrico Ripandelli.

PRODUCTION AND EXPORT

Between 2,000 and 2,500 L3 fast tanks were built, of all the models and variants described. Many foreign countries bought it in different versions. At the time, the construction of a CV33 cost around 86,800 lire, the equivalent of 90,000 euros today –in short, a cheap weapon.

• Afghanistan: an unknown number of CV35s between 1937 and 1939.

• Albania: six tanks in 1938.

• Austria: 72 tanks, 36 CV33 2nd series (in 1935) and 36 CV35 1st series (in 1937). All the tanks for the Austrian army were rearmed with an 8 mm Schwarzlose machine gun.

• Bolivia: a series of radio-equipped tanks between 1937 and 1938.

• Brazil: 23 CV35 II series, of which five were armed with 13.2 mm Breda machine guns and eighteen with two Madsen cal. 7 binate Mauser. However, the Brazilians seem to have benefited from the delivery of a few L3/38s.

• Bulgaria: 10 CV33 I series armed with Schwartzlose machine guns (1933).

• China: almost a hundred tanks between L3/33 and L3.35, whose armament underwent several modifications.

• Nationalist Spain: some vehicles used during the Spanish Civil War were later integrated into the Spanish army.

• Hungary: a large but inaccurate number of CV35 tanks were assembled in series with Brno 26 machine guns. Some pictures show that the Hungarians made modifications to the hatch.

• Iraq: some models sold in 1938 to the Iraqi armed forces.

Other vehicles were sold to Greece and Paraguay, the latter used them during the Chaco War.

MAJOR USER

The L3 was used by all its purchasers, but obviously its main user was Mussolini's fascist Italy, in the Regio Esercito above all, but also, after the Armistice, by the Esercito Nazionale Repubblicano and the Guardia Nazionale Repubblicana, following the establishment of the Italian Social Republic in 1943. As early as 1935, the Ethiopians captured a few light fast tanks. Several L3s were also captured and reused by the Greeks during the Greek-Italian War of 1940-1941. After the invasion of Yugoslavia and the Battle of Greece (1941), many L3s were also captured and re-used by Yugoslav partisans and the Greek resistance. From 1941, some L3s were handed over by the Germans to the puppet government of the independent state of Croatia (*Nezavisna Država Hrvatska*, or NDH). Some of these vehicles remained in service in Italy for a short time during the post-war years, as part of police missions.

▲ 35 Fiat Ansaldo CV33 of the Bulgarian army in 1936. (Wikipedia).

▼ CV L 35 used in the Spanish Civil War and later repainted in the new Nationalist Army (Wikipedia).

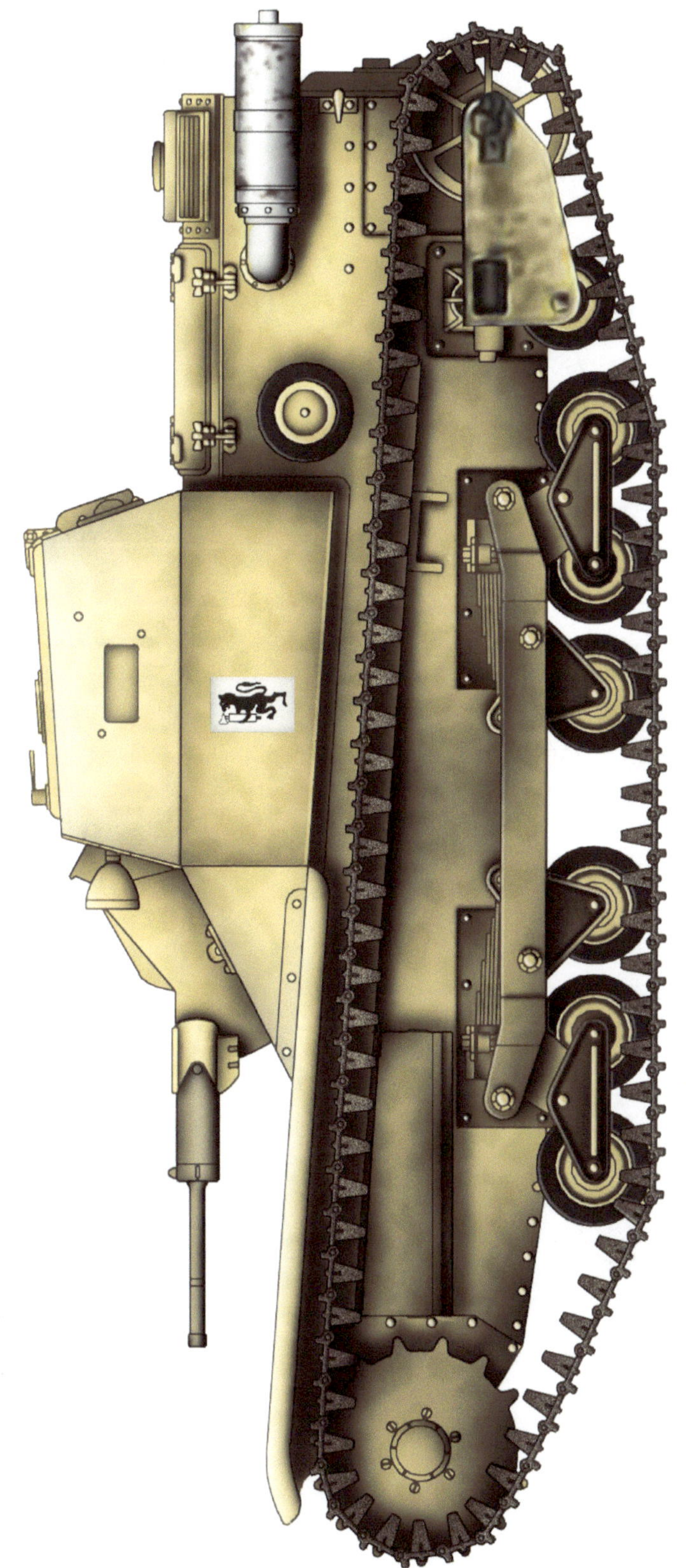

▲ 1944-45, hypothetical reconstruction of a light tank belonging to the Leoncello Group. A department that has always aroused curiosity and interest, the "Leoncello" Armored Group was one of the few armored units of the Italian Social Republic, the only one of the Tanker specialty.

▲ CV33 of the 3rd Battalion of the 31st Tank Regiment in Montenegro. (Bundesarchiv).

▼ Another picture of CV33 of the 3rd Battalion of the 31st Tank Regiment in Montenegro. (Bundesarchiv).

FAST TANKS IN THE ITALIAN CIVIL WAR 1943-1945

▲ 1944: L3/35 Flamethrower of the "San Giusto" Armored Group, equipped with a homemade tank for flammable liquid, placed on the engine hood.

	CV33	CV35	CV38
Length	3150 mm	3150 mm	3150 mm
Width	1400 mm	1400 mm	1400 mm
Height	1287 mm	1300 mm	1350 mm
Height above ground	230 mm	250 mm	280 mm
Weight in combat order	3200 kg	3500 kg	3500 kg
Crew	2	2	2
Engine	CV 3-05 gasoline 4 cylinder of 2745 cm3 , developing 43 hp at 2400 rpm		
Maximum speed	42 km/h on road 14 km/h off road	42 km/h on road 14 km/h off road	42 km/h on road 20 km/h off road
Range	150 km on road 6 h off road	150 km on road 6 h off road	150 km on road 6 h off road
Tank capacity	62 L	62 L	62 L
Armor thickness	From 6 to 14 mm	From 6 to 15 mm	From 6 to 15 mm
Armament	1st Series: 1 Fiat 14 6.5 mm machine gun (3800 rounds) 2nd Series: 2 Fiat 14/35 8 mm machine guns (2480 rounds)	2 Fiat 14/35 8 mm machine guns (2480 rounds) or 2 Breda 38 8 mm machine guns (1896 rounds)	2 Breda 38 8 mm machine guns (1896 rounds)

▼ Some L tanks and a self-propelled tank at a partisan parade at the end of the war. Author's coloration.

FAST TANKS IN THE ITALIAN CIVIL WAR 1943-1945

▲ Spring 1944: L3/38 used in Valsesia by the 1st Assault Legion "Tagliamento" of the Republican National Guard.

▲ Captain Crippa's CV33 slaughtered in Dembeguina (Ethiopia 1935). Author collection.

▼ Another image of CV33s surrounded by mechanics in the Scyre (Ethiopia), October 1935 (Author Collection).

FAST TANKS IN THE ITALIAN CIVIL WAR 1943-1945

R. Calò

▲ December 1944: L3/35 of the Mobile Autonomous Legion "Ettore Muti" of Milan.

FAST TANKS IN THE ITALIAN CIVIL WAR 1943-1945

▲ Fall 1944: light tank of the Anti-Partisan Grouping in Piedmont: this is an L3/33, brought up to the standards of an L3/38.

R. Calo'

FAST TANKS IN THE ITALIAN CIVIL WAR 1943-1945

▲ April 1945: L3 of R.A.P. Light Tank Company stationed in Alba, captured by partisans at the end of the war. Under the handmade inscription "II DIV. LANGHE" it is still possible to see the Republican tricolor, which was placed on almost all armored vehicles of the Anti-Partisan Regiment.

BIBLIOGRAPHY

- *Gli autoveicoli da combattimento dell'Esercito Italiano, Volume primo (dalle origini fino al 1939)*, Nicola Pignato & Filippo Cappellano, Stato Maggiore dell'Esercito, Ufficio Storico, 2002
- *Carro L3, Carri Veloci, Carri Leggeri, derivati*, Andrea Tallillo, Antonio Tallillo & Daniele Guglielmi, GMT, 2004
- *Carri leggeri, carro veloce 33-35 - evoluzione del mezzo*, Carri Armati 2/I, Aldo Cumbo, Fronte Terra, Edizioni Bizzarri 1973
- *Carri leggeri, carro veloce 33-35 - le operazioni belliche*, Carri Armati 2/II, Aldo Cumbo, Fronte Terra, Edizioni Bizzarri 1973
- *C.V. 33/35*, Janusz Ledwoch, Wydawnictwo Militaria, 2009
- *I reparti corazzati italiani nei Balcani*, Paolo Crippa e Carlo Cucut. Soldiershop 2019
- *I reparti corazzati del R.E. E l'armistizio 1° Volume*, Paolo Crippa. Soldiershop 2021
- *I reparti corazzati del R.E. E l'armistizio 2° Volume*, Paolo Crippa. Soldiershop 2021
- *Il gruppo corazzato del Leoncello*, Paolo Crippa. Soldiershop 2021
- *I mezzi blindo-corazzati italiani 1923-1943*, Nicola Pignato, Storia Militare, 2005
- *Corazzati Italiani 1939-1945*, Nico Sgarlato, War Set n°10, 2006
- *Mezzi dell'Esercito Italiano 1935-45*, Ugo Barlozzetti & Alberto Pirella, Editoriale Olimpia, 1986
- *Corazzati e blindati italiani dalle origini allo scoppio della seconda guerra mondiale*, David Vannucci, Editrice Innocenti, 2003
- *Articolo di* Cédric Mas, Batailles & Blindés n°13-14, 2006
- *Carro veloce Ansaldo Fiat tipo C.V. 33* , Genova 1935
- *Nozioni sull'uso l'impiego e la manutenzione del carro veloce L3*. Torino 1938
- *Le fiamme rosse del 31° Reggimento Carristi*, Maurizio Parri, Soldiershop, 2021
- *Il gruppo corazzato "San Giusto" dal Regio Esercito alla RSI 1934-1945*, Stefano Di Giusto, Laran Éditions, 2008
- *I reparti corazzati della Repubblica Sociale Italiana 1943/1945*, Paolo Crippa, Marvia Edizioni, 2006
- *...Come il diamante, I Carrisit italiani 1943-45*, Sergio Corbatti & Marco Nava, Laran Edizioni, 2008
- *Alle origini della Breda Meccanica Bresciana*, A. Curami, P. Ferrari & A. Rastelli, Fondazione Negri, 2009
- *Storia dell'Ansaldo 6. Dall'IRI alla guerra 1930-1945*, Gabriele De Rosa, Gius. Laterza & Figli, 1999

BOOKS AVAILABLE

TWE-001 EN

9 788889 327866